WEEKLY **WR** READER®
EARLY LEARNING LIBRARY

Nature's Food Chains

What
Polar Animals Eat

by Joanne Mattern

Reading consultant: Susan Nations, M.Ed.,
author/literacy coach/consultant
Science and curriculum consultant: Debra Voege, M.A.,
science and math curriculum resource teacher

Please visit our web site at: www.garethstevens.com
For a free color catalog describing Weekly Reader® Early Learning Library's list
of high-quality books, call 1-877-445-5824 (USA) or 1-800-387-3178 (Canada).
Weekly Reader® Early Learning Library's fax: (414) 336-0164.

Library of Congress Cataloging-in-Publication Data

Mattern, Joanne, 1963-
    What polar animals eat / by Joanne Mattern.
        p. cm. — (Nature's food chains)
    Includes bibliographical references and index.
    ISBN-10: 0-8368-6873-0 — ISBN-13: 978-0-8368-6873-9 (lib. bdg.)
    ISBN-10: 0-8368-6880-3 — ISBN-13: 978-0-8368-6880-7 (softcover)
    1. Animals—Polar regions—Food—Juvenile literature.   2. Food chains (Ecology)—
Juvenile literature.   I. Title.   II. Series: Mattern, Joanne, 1963- Nature's food chains.
QL104.M38   2007
591.75'86—dc22   2006009182

This edition first published in 2007 by
Weekly Reader® Early Learning Library
A Member of the WRC Media Family of Companies
330 West Olive Street, Suite 100
Milwaukee, WI 53212 USA

Editor: Barbara Kiely Miller
Art direction: Tammy West
Cover design, page layout, and illustrations: Dave Kowalski
Picture research: Diane Laska-Swanke

Picture credits: Cover, title, © Hans Strand/CORBIS; p. 5 © Steven Kazlowski/SeaPics.com;
p. 7 © Peter Parks/iq3-d/SeaPics.com; p. 9 © David Tipling/naturepl.com; pp. 11, 13 © Florian Graner/
SeaPics.com; p. 15 © Mats Forsberg/naturepl.com; p. 17 © Doc White/SeaPics.com;
p. 19 © Robert L. Pitman/SeaPics.com

Printed in the United States of America

1 2 3 4 5 6 7 8 9 10 09 08 07 06

Note to Educators and Parents

Reading is such an exciting adventure for young children! They are beginning to integrate their oral language skills with written language. To encourage children along the path to early literacy, books must be colorful, engaging, and interesting; they should invite the young reader to explore both the print and the pictures.

The *Nature's Food Chains* series is designed to help children learn about the interrelationships between animals in a food chain. In each book, young readers will learn interesting facts about what animals eat in different habitats and how food chains are connected into food webs.

Each book is specially designed to support the young reader in the reading process. The familiar topics are appealing to young children and invite them to read — and reread — again and again. The full-color photographs and enhanced text further support the student during the reading process.

In addition to serving as wonderful picture books in schools, libraries, homes, and other places where children learn to love reading, these books are specifically intended to be read within an instructional guided reading group. This small group setting allows beginning readers to work with a fluent adult model as they make meaning from the text. After children develop fluency with the text and content, the book can be read independently. Children and adults alike will find these books supportive, engaging, and fun!

— Susan Nations, M.Ed., author, literacy coach,
and consultant in literacy development

All living things need food to live and grow. Many animals eat plants. Some eat smaller animals. These **walruses** are part of a **polar** food chain. A **food chain** shows the order of who eats what.

Plants are at the bottom of polar food chains. They make their own food from sunshine, water, and air. At the North Pole, some plants live in the ocean. These plants are called **plankton**.

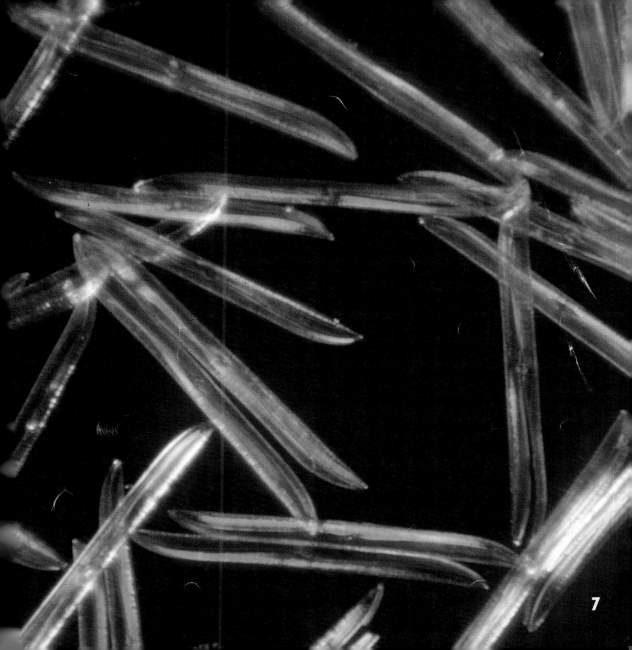

7

Small fish eat the plankton. Fish
must eat a lot of plankton to live.

FOOD CHAIN

Small Fish

Plankton

9

Bigger fish eat the small fish.

This **cod** eats small fish.

FOOD CHAIN

Cod

↑

Small Fish

↑

Plankton

Many big polar animals eat fish.
This **seal** eats a fish.

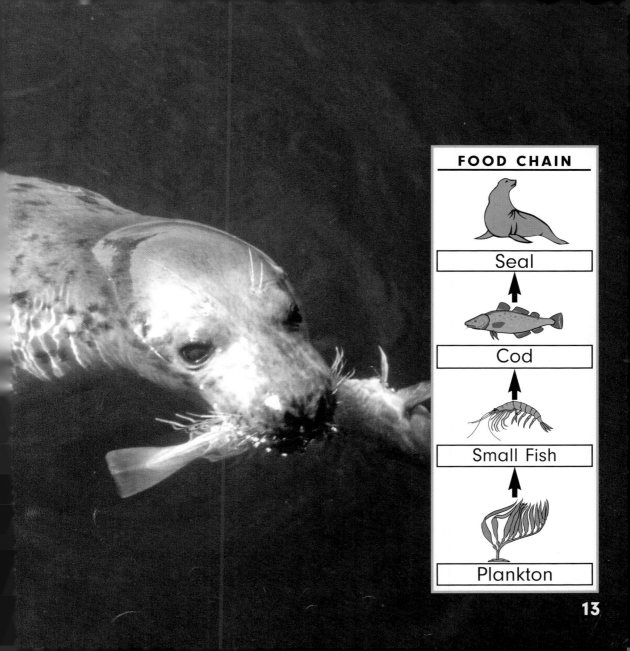

FOOD CHAIN

Seal

↑

Cod

↑

Small Fish

↑

Plankton

Then a bigger animal may eat the seal. This polar bear wants to eat a seal. Polar bears are at the top of their food chains. No other animals eat them.

FOOD CHAIN

Polar Bear

Seal

Cod

Small Fish

Plankton

Polar areas have many food chains.

Large animals eat plankton, too.

A walrus eats lots of plankton.

FOOD CHAIN

Walrus

↑

Plankton

Then a whale may eat the walrus. This whale eats seals, too. They are at the top of many polar food chains. Eating many foods helps animals stay alive.

FOOD CHAIN

Whale

↑

Walrus

↑

Plankton

19

A **food web** is formed when two or more food chains are **connected**. Animals that are part of more than one food chain connect the chains. Food webs show that animals have many things to eat!

A Polar Food Web

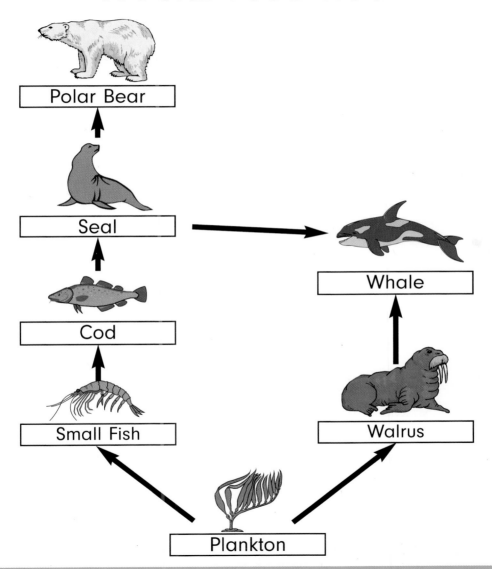

Glossary

food chain — a list of living things, in which each plant or animal is eaten by the next animal on the list

food web — food chains that are connected by a plant or animal that is common to both chains

North Pole — the most northern part of Earth

plankton — very tiny sea plants

polar — having to do with the North Pole or the South Pole

For More Information

Books

A Killer Whale's World. Caroline Arnold's Animals (series).
  Caroline Arnold (Picture Window Books)

Killer Whales. See More Readers (series). Seymour Simon
  (Chronicle Books)

The Life Cycle of a Polar Bear. The Life Cycle (series).
  Rebecca Sjonger (Crabtree Publishing)

Walruses. Early Bird Nature Books (series).
  Frank J. Staub   (Lerner)

Web Site

Polar Bears
www.seaworld.org/animal-info/info-books/polar-bear/
Lots of information about polar bears, plus fun activities
and information about other polar animals

Publisher's note to educators and parents: Our editors have carefully reviewed this
Web site to ensure that it is suitable for children. Many Web sites change frequently,
however, and we cannot guarantee that a site's future contents will continue to meet
our high standards of quality and educational value. Be advised that children should
be closely supervised whenever they access the Internet.

Index

About the Author

Joanne Mattern has written more than one hundred and fifty books for children. Joanne also works in her local library. She lives in New York State with her husband, three daughters, and assorted pets. She enjoys animals, music, going to baseball games, reading, and visiting schools to talk about her books.